# The Rise of a Woman

# The Rise of a Woman

Rhiannon Janae

The Rise of a Woman

@rhiannonjanaepoetry

**ISBN:** 9798323098637

*This book is dedicated to anyone who has ever felt small.*

*I hope you rise higher than the skies and roar louder than the lions.*

*It is with our voices we will finally be heard.*

*'Trigger Warning'*

*This book talks about mental illness, grief, death, substance abuse, depression, childhood trauma, and abuse.*

*This is an extremely vulnerable experience.*

*The intention of this publication is to help others find comfort in the imperfections.*

*And maybe it was the battles she overcame that made her so beautiful.*

# Contents

The Leftovers of a Lover

## The Rise of a Woman

Flux inside of me.
I yearn to be poisoned.
It's all I was ever taught to love.

Rhiannon Janae

The first sip stung.
I never liked the taste of red wine until you
poured me some.
The glass filled, repeatedly.
Every breath felt lighter with each sip.
You lit me up
while my lungs decayed from all the smoke we
inhaled.

But each drag kept me feeling closer to you.
Your smile told me what your heart couldn't.
I knew you were the beat to my incomplete
rhythm, and as the night turned over, so did my
stomach.

Cheap wine wasn't drinking me the same.
I held back as long as I could,
choking down the insecurities,
but the inevitable crawled up through me like a
spider.
You held my hair
and the warmth of your hands whispered that
this was the start of cheap wine, cigarettes, and
unrequited love.

*-our first date*

# The Rise of a Woman

We were aligned; two parallels
drifting into unknown space.
Your hands clenched
the goodness you buried,
holding onto me
like a diamond you resurfaced.
You told me I was precious,
like something rare wrapped in humanity,
enticing me with poisonous kisses.
The kind of kisses that make your lips swell and
leave you crippling for more.

White lace hung solemnly around my waist, pressing up against the spots you loved. I wore my best only to grow numb. Your empty promises lured me in. When one broke, another one would bloom. Your words had been lingering and smoldering inside of me. In and out just like you said, coaxing me through all my rapid heartbeats. You swore to me that they would never kill me, only leave me in a trance I will never understand. I sat there, trembling in white lace, rocking back and forth in your arms, as you rubbed your palms up and down my chest. I sat there calm, yet frightened. Then the moment evaporated, leaving my white lace to shed into nothing but scraps.

## The Rise of a Woman

I am your neglectful mother.
I am your sick father.
I am your childhood trauma.
I am your failed education.
I am your lost years from incarceration.
I am the rage you hide inside of your chest.
I am everything you hate about yourself,
and all I wanted was to be your love.

*-I am not the problem*

Rhiannon Janae

Your words hung heavy in my mouth as I spat
them back out at you.

I never learned when to hold back.

## The Rise of a Woman

January bites hard.
My withered body can barely hold my bones.
My faults hate me,
this grey eyed burden.
A pale goddess he says,
but who is he?

He holds me under textured quilts.
He kisses my chewed-up cheeks.
He holds my hand to let others know I'm 'his'.

"Wake up!" I say to myself,
"This is all a fabrication."
I watch the blue daises rot in our bedroom as he
wrongs me again.
I cry, but not for him.
I cry only for her; the one I have lost inside of
this skin I wear.

*-20's are for wilting*

Rhiannon Janae

I said I want to feel all that makes me wild
and taste all that makes me weak.
And then you came along.

*-be careful what you wish for*

## The Rise of a Woman

It's so lovely how you dance with The Devil
as his smile wraps you up in blue.
I came with swords of worry
but he was much too strong for me to get
through.

Your blue has me begging
for our retired innocence
that we have lost along the way.
My thoughts are about our old tiny kisses,
the ones that sit in jars that now decay.

Dear, I know my tears don't mind you.
I have wet these pages under many moons.
My screams won't find you anymore
since The Devil has wrapped you in *blue.*

-*The Devil that wore blue*

Rhiannon Janae

I've got sin all over my lips
from all the lies your kisses have left.

-*lips of a liar*

## The Rise of a Woman

You removed my insides and replaced them with your own. My heart was always yours, you claimed. Your claw marks never released my heart you gripped onto. You loved me because you wanted me to be all the things you never had, when in fact, I was all the things you hated. You saw me as the one who had ruined you when you had blood on your hands. My voice wasn't mine; it was your mother's as she left another man in your house to beat the child out of you. My love was the death of your father that you kept burrowed inside of your stomach, only to purge it out with sickness in the morning. I was not the one you loved. I was everything you hated. And that's why you never stopped taking from me. I was a doormat clinging to your footsteps and calling it love. I was everyone you hated and that was how you loved me.

*-the trauma that grew you into a 'man'*

My hands try to fix people who let their wounds bleed all over me. I clean off the blood and wipe my hands, then watch as they go to try and patch their wounds all over again.

*-when will I ever learn?*

## The Rise of a Woman

To fall asleep
without your hands
creeping inside
the hollowness of the
temple I live in.
You try to wreck it
after you set fire to your own.
But my skin is a lot tougher
than the coward you hide inside of.

Rhiannon Janae

Shackled
to his waist,
I became a vision
of hate inside of the mirror.
"Who is she?"
My eyes showered over my glued shut lips.

His voice growling out,
"She is mine."
My ears ringing
from the voice who couldn't shield away from
the war he had dragged me into.

"She is mine."
he repeats.
And wasn't she?

She did not hold the key to those chains she
swelled inside of.

*-swallow her whole*

*Your words were so
soothing.*

*If only your hands had
learned
from your mouth.*

Rhiannon Janae

I always love the ones who never seem to love
themselves.

I love to study tragedy.

*A mirror of myself.*

## The Rise of a Woman

**A Sacrifice.**

**An offering**

*from whom she belongs to.*
*To place her in hands that can't hold her.*

**A reckoning.**

**An affair**

*of two people choosing to love one another more than*
*the ones they are inside of.*

**A disaster.**

**A destruction**.

*It never ends well when the stranger you have*
*become to yourself tries to fix your lover.*

*-too broken to love*

I remember meeting him.
He spoke,

*"I lost my father."*

I gasped,

*"I lost my mother."*

Was it God?
Was it meant to be?

Two broken people.
A beautiful tragedy.

But the problem is when you
love someone who is broken
that does not want to be fixed,
*it all ends in pieces.*

## The Rise of a Woman

Twenty-third of December.
Cobwebs cover my mouth
as the spiders wrap themselves around me.

It feels like some kind of warped comfort.

My voice speaks, but no one listens
to the cries of intuition
that feed my bones.

Lights on, no-one home
but grief nesting itself inside of me.


*-the day I lost you*

*The grief inside of me burrows so deep that my organs dance in mourning of who they used to be.*

## The Rise of a Woman

He was masked as my lover,
lies spilling out of his lips.
His piercing eyes held secrets
of desperate woman unzipping his jeans,
kneeling like servants
as he convinced himself he was king.
The only thing he reigned over
was a grieving woman who just lost her **queen**.

*-the loss of my mother turned me into his lover*

Rhiannon Janae

I am wreckage.
Leftovers from a man
whose palate is never satisfied.
Feeding off women
like some sort of mixed fruit.
Sweet, yet never sweet enough.
The hunger is never quite filling,
the filling is never quite pleasing.
Just endless amounts of choosing.
But I am always kept, never thrown away.
I am just leftovers that always make the cut
to be kept so the hunger
can be filled,
temporarily.
The only woman who
he sinks his teeth into repeatedly.

I am leftovers,
but never thrown away.
But leftovers go bad
**and I can feel a sickness inside of me.**

*-a brewing of redemption*

## The Rise of a Woman

The Sun king was threatening,
devouring me wholly.
I was endangered, scuffed,
shouting out for my freedom.
He wrapped me in thorns,
pouring out drops of my innocence.
I was calm but silenced.
*I cried for years.*

Rhiannon Janae

*My old lover held so many hearts caged inside of him, that he couldn't remember their names or whose heart belonged to whom.*

*-heart-keeper*

## The Rise of a Woman

Sticks and stones will break my bones
and your words eat at me.
Through my flesh,
rubbing the bone,
reminding me of who I will never be
and how hard I am to love.

I am a burden.
I am a burden.
But he won't let me go.
I am a burden.
I am a burden.
But he claims to love me so.
I am a burden.
I am his burden
to show.

Rhiannon Janae

The man I loved like a God
took his hands,
raised me above the floor,
back and ribs against the wall.
My body's silhouette carved its outings inside.
Feet dangled,
eyes spilled
*as I lost my religion.*

*-no God, no sins*

## The Rise of a Woman

I waited until the walls grew mold.
You grew, yet I broke.
My shattered pieces sliced my every step.
I fell over, shedding nothing but tears.
My mind shut off like an unplugged television.
White noise only played to my ears.
My voice screamed at the silence,
louder and louder to drown it out.
I only wanted you.

*I'll be waiting like a pile of bones that someone*
*might recover,*
*and if they do,*
*they can put me next to yours.*
*Then I can become calm,*
*and this disaster growing inside can devour me.*
*We can walk to the ocean*
*and you can throw me in the waves like you used to.*
*The fall won't hurt since I am deceased.*
*You will just stare into me*
*and tell me how you never meant to leave.*

*-the waves and the wishing*

It makes me sick,
how rotten my insides
became
just from loving you.

## The Rise of a Woman

I once loved with all of me.
My insides, dying for him.
Condemned,
fluxing.
My heart, his apple.
Biting hard
into my innocence
as it dripped from his mouth.
I once loved with all of me
and that was **enough.**

Rhiannon Janae

You try to break me,
but all that pours out
are stories of a woman who has let love drown
her.

You try to break me,
but all that is shown is
pictures of a mother
who was too sick to care for her own.

You try to break me,
but all my pieces will show you how hard I have
fought to stay inside of myself.

You try to break me,
but the wars that grow inside of me have taught
me how to become friends with the battles at
large.

You try to break me,
yet I stay resilient
and all that floods the floor is the hatred you
have become inside.

You try to break me,
but it doesn't reflect.
My mirror stays true of a woman who always
rises from below no matter how hard it is to
swim.

## The Rise of a Woman

You try to break me,
but all you do is break yourself.

*-don't take what isn't yours*

Rhiannon Janae

*There are stories inside of me that haunt me. Words that bruise me, echoes that taunt me. I am a woman full of grief. I am renewed, but when will I be restored? A haunting of a life that has lived.*

The Rise of a Woman

Harvest me
somewhere inside of your skin
or soul
so that I can last
beyond my earthly years.

Remember me
somewhere inside of your ears
or conscious
so that you know where to find me.
Over and over,
life after life.

Maybe we are one
life away
from getting it right.

*-the many lives, the many mistakes*

The day I almost chose to die. It was cold or maybe hot. I couldn't tell from all the cheap wine rushing to my face. I was numb but it was normal. Just another day of feeling hopeless in a home that was meant for more. I was sick, starving for my body to take away the grief that grew inside. It was becoming bigger. I kept hoping it would just swallow me. But I kept waking up in a home full of misery. I missed him. The one I had spent the last five years loving. The one who knew what it was like to feel betrayed by life. If I could just get back to him, then I could be home again. So, I left, the door slamming behind and decided to walk toward where the water lay under the bridge. If I could just walk myself up there and jump, then maybe he would catch me in the water, and I would be enveloped by something other than my grief. But before I could get there, I could hear a ringing from inside of my pocket. A miracle if I ever heard one. I answered. Her voice reminded me that someone might want me here. A friend, a friendly reminder. My feet started slightly turning around. I walked and decided to never look back or think about the water under the bridge. What a silly thing for me to forget how much I hate swimming.

## The Rise of a Woman

I ran to the city to run away from all the pain the suburbs spewed. You followed behind slowly after me. I grew hope in that tiny apartment. Every picture I hung up, I could see our love blossoming in the reflection. But the problem is, I have always had an imagination like wildflowers growing inside of me so rapidly that I can't see reality. All that home saw was loss. The loss that bled out through my stomach and down my legs. The one thing you wanted more than anything. The loss of watching your mind eat away at itself, leaving the man I had fallen in love with vacant. The loss of watching you walk out that door, knowing deep down inside of me, it was the last time anyone would ever see you again. Now I have run away from the pain of the city and back to the suburbs where this all started. But here, I decided to start over again. **Alone**.

*-finding the parts of me I had lost*

Rhiannon Janae

Loving you was chaos
wrapped in sweet lips that I craved
under yellow skies and midnight blues.

Loving you was hypnotic
but I gladly walked the tight rope,
knowing just beneath me
was tragedy waiting to catch my fall.

Loving you was endless
even through death
beyond these years,
**you call to me.**

*-the dimension between us*

# The Rise of a Woman

*I could not fix you, but I tried.*

My hands bled as you squeezed
your hidden lies inside of them.

*I could not fix you, but I tried.*

My legs ached from carrying you
and your sickness for so long.

*I could not fix you, but I tried.*

My ears swelled from the constant
degradation you spoke into them.

*I could not fix you, but I tried.*

My mind bruised from the way
you made me feel so unloved,
as you grew more hate for yourself
inside.

*I could not fix you,
but I can fix me
if only I just try.*

*-three strikes, I'm out*

Rhiannon Janae

I whisper to the wind
in hopes that the breeze will reach you.
My voice travels to soothe the graves
I have grown inside of me.
It is all dirt, despite shoveling it out,
it just becomes deeper,
like my love for you.
Deep like graves
and endless immortality.
Despite all that has happened,
I still whisper to the wind
in hopes that the breeze will reach you.

*In hopes that I will soon be released.*

## The Rise of a Woman

These roots intertwine through me.
*I evolve*, becoming the true me.
I was made from this soil, drowning in the rain
to absorb my thirst.
The sunlight strengthens my bones.
The moonlight kisses me to slumber.
I am the ground you walked on,
the petals you ripped apart,
**the woman you took for granted.**

*-through the soil she will grow*

Rhiannon Janae

The black ink on my wrist
leaves me reminiscing in the pain of loving you.

A reminder of the girl who fell in love with a
disaster of a man and was left with nothing but
ashes and bone.

I have a box of abandonment that holds pages
of your lies that entice the parts of me
that are trying to let go.

He did not love me,
but he loved the way I made him feel.

I did love him,
but I did not love the way he made me feel.

How does that work? You may wonder.

It doesn't.

**It doesn't.**

## The Rise of a Woman

*I am not bitter of love.*

*I am just resistant to fall into such a dangerous thing again.*

You can call it terminal, but don't call it a weakness. You've pressed all the soft spots that have grown inside of me and left your handprints. But I am no longer ashamed of loving you. I think it just shows my strength and the fact that my heart is so pure that it can still fit you inside of all the places that you broke.

*-in remission*

## The Rise of a Woman

*I thought my heart would forever bleed for you.*

*A wound left untreated,*
*unrequited love,*
*desired death.*

*But all along,*

*my heart was meant to beat inside*
*the chest of a woman*
*you never deserved in the first place.*

Rhiannon Janae

I created an ocean with all the tears I've cried for you. And despite all the years of treading in its waves of grief, I have finally learned to let the waves carry me.

*-the salt no longer stings*

## The Rise of a Woman

When the years pass and the death fades,
you become a fever dream.
One I barely see.

*A time capsule, a memory loss.*

How could you have once taken up all of my
head and now you are barely a thought?

*It's a blessing, a ritual.*

I must go on inside
of a space that no longer holds you.
But I will wait until my head feels hot
and my eyes fall heavy.

*In this fever, will we reminisce with each other.*

*-fever dream*

Rhiannon Janae

I dug it out,
the remembrance of my past.
It sat deep inside of my stomach
because of the way I was raised.
Quiet, as it pulled me apart.
I wanted it all, I wanted it all out of me.
It hung in my hands,
the chokehold of codependency.
I pushed; I pulled it out of me.
Tell me now, what do you see?

A woman of truth?
A woman of sacrifice?
**A woman who no longer needs you.**

The Bloodline, The Chain

## The Rise of a Woman

Words to my parents:

*When you chose not to heal, your toxicity polluted the whole sea.*

*-all three of us*

Rhiannon Janae

Childhood was four walls with a silence only
the sound of my guitar could fill. Or the way
my voice cracked as I sang off key. How all the
other children would sit on wood during the
week as their minds rejected knowledge. But I
sat only within my four walls in a home my
parents accepted from the hands of my mother's
father. The very father who shrieked violence
when the whiskey filled his blood stream. The
violence my mother never healed from. The
lack of healing she hid from behind me, her
favorite child out of all three. The child that sat
in that home, bearing all the burdens, all her
mother's burdens.

*I'm a prisoner with no charge.*

*A sack of bones in varnished flesh,*

*walking around hoping somebody will root me.*

*–unrooted*

Rhiannon Janae

In this home

we aren't scared of love.

It is the worry that it isn't here at all.

# The Rise of a Woman

A child, silent.

Words not spoken unless her mother whispered them beforehand.

A child,

shameful with lies on her hands, tears spilling out from her eyes, pleading to just go outside like the others.

Get me out of these brown walls filled with a woman who wants to help me.

Get these lies off my tongue that fall out of my mother's mouth.

I am not a liar.

They will see that when I look down at my hands and try to swallow my words back.

She did not hurt me, the girl, my friend that my mother took away.

This is all a projection.

This is all control that my mother releases onto me.

She is sick.
She is collapsing and contorting me to live in
her memories.

I am not sick.
I am still pure.

The insides of my legs have never been torn.

I am not hurt.
I am not broken.
I am not my mother, just my mother's child.

*-Munchausen syndrome*

## The Rise of a Woman

*This home is not a safe zone.*

*It holds violence and repression*

*of untreated trauma from adults looking*

*to pass it on to the ones whom they made.*

*How are we so young, but feel so heavy?*

*How can you sleep, knowing we are wide awake?*

*-sleep paralysis*

Rhiannon Janae

Childhood.
The isolation of my bedroom
that peeked over the neighborhood
at children who got to play and learn.
I felt secluded,
like a hidden secret nobody knew.
This child who was me,
was kept in these walls,
consuming my mother's teachings
with books that stopped in the age range of
where her childhood trauma began.
I was soaked in nursery rhymes
and all ages of stories.
My brain craved knowledge, friendship, and
youth.
But I sat there inside my bedroom walls,
peeking over the neighborhood
at the children that got to play,
as all I did was grow
**faster than them all.**

*-the home, the school, the loneliness*

The Rise of a Woman

I am *sorrow.*

I am the daughter of the one I fear.
I am the child of unspoken trauma.

I am *sorrow.*

I am broken insides.
I am cherished evil.
I am seduced by danger.

I am s*orrow.*

Rhiannon Janae

I do not know what love is because all those
who loved me the most have given me nothing
more than pain.

## The Rise of a Woman

My child hands were so small.

*So why did you put such a heavy burden inside of them?*

*-hands full of generations*

*A child should not bear the trauma of the ones who brought them into this world.*

## The Rise of a Woman

*The morning.*

*The night.*

*The light of the unforgiving.*

*I am a mirror*

*of a future*

*I must resist.*

*A strength that exhausts.*

*A child that must fight for herself*

*harder than the ones that are in charge.*

*-mirror, mirror*

Rhiannon Janae

Mocking me, she denies my help
as I watch her wilt away into debris,
flaking off suddenly.
Her smile becomes my concern,
teeth shattering together to get that last bite.
I clench my hands with defeat,
gasping endless pleads for her to just open her
ears.
Hear my words as they coax her monster,
but they evaporate as soon as they hit the air.
Her denial
becomes my fear.

*Was it her sickness?*
*Or was it the pills?*

*-which one took her away?*

## The Rise of a Woman

Whenever I saw my mother
swallowing a pill,
I imagined it was a seed
that would eventually bloom
inside of her *stomach.*

*-the flowers never came*

Rhiannon Janae

Her yellow hair fell just mid-back,
splitting at the edges.
Her smile was white,
but lying behind melancholia.
Her kisses on my head were demands,
whispering taunts disguised as love.
I listened.
**I ate the fruit**.
I let her entice me with false reasonings,
dwelling on irrational decisions,
swerving around destructive thoughts.
I just wanted a hero,
even if it was all a fabrication.

*-the mother, the apple, the poison*

## The Rise of a Woman

It started with a diet
taught to me by the woman
who held me in her womb.

The woman I now feel empty without.

The woman who kept me close
and taught me how to be the thinnest in the
room.

*It started with a diet*
*and ended with my bones and psyche decaying.*

*-the start of a sickness*

Rhiannon Janae

Mother kept me so close
because she thought
the *closer*, the *better*
her protection could keep me.
But the closer she got,
I felt more of her
*daggers,*
*wounds,*
*and scars*
appearing on **my** skin.

*-her wounds, my skin*

The Rise of a Woman

*Mother.*

*Were you toxic?*

*Or just intoxicated?*

Rhiannon Janae

She was sick, but she was a mother.

The woman who untangled my knots
after I played mermaid in the bath.

The woman who wiped the chocolate
off my mouth as it slowly consumed my chin.

The woman who clasped me in her embrace
after monsters invaded my sleep.

*She was sick, but she was a mother.*

*-my mother*

## The Rise of a Woman

Death and I first met in August
when she overcame my mother.

I saw her in my mother's blanched skin
and heard her in the silence of the air,
the white noise that drowned my ears.

Death told me
that she would return.

And ever since,
She's all I think about.

*-the day my brain broke obsessively, compulsively*

*To be mother-less*

is like riding a bike with no brakes and learning
how to put your feet down at the right moment
for safety.

*To be mother-less*

is like road tripping across the country with a
blank map that needs you to create the way
with all the right directions.

*To be mother-less*

is like planting a seed inside of yourself and
being expected to learn how to water it
properly for it to grow.

*To be mother-less*

is to feel directionless.

## The Rise of a Woman

I was a clone,
a reset
that she birthed
like a button
she had been waiting
to press.
Her pride,
her joy,
her second chance.
But all she birthed
was a burden
that I carry.

*So, I seal my legs closed*
*to not let this burden*
*be rebirthed from me.*

*-childless*

A crime.

I am guilty.

I have become my own burden,
punishing myself for years.

Starving my own bones
as if that would take my mother's sickness away
from her.

But all that came of it
was a **brewing**,
a **breeding**
of sickness that I had let grow inside of me.

## The Rise of a Woman

I have found myself here,
webbing through life,
obsessively resisting
the pattern of becoming my mother.

Now I find myself
empty handed, forgetful
of how to become myself.

*-lost in translation*

I was made from my parents' love in a home full of hate. The middle of three children who did not ask to be bargained. Three children who could not maintain our mother's sick mind or see how our father fell into regression. Three children who grew up too fast, only to revert as we got older. To have children is to be able to hold someone in your hands that you would give your life for. Now we are three children, fighting for the life we were never given.

-*starting from the beginning*

## The Rise of a Woman

I have become an abyss,
an endless grieving maw
that swallows me whole.

Do not ask me to save you.
I am no savior.
*I have death on my hands.*

*-all the ones I couldn't fix*

Rhiannon Janae

The womb she carried us in was once a home
for our growth.

Now our growth has been stunted from the
home we live in.

If only we could have stayed in her womb, the
only safe home we've ever lived in.

*–before it was loud, it was silent*

## The Rise of a Woman

Mother's casket.

Rose embroidered,

sweetly sealed with a wooden brush.

Latches closed to conceal her vacant soul
covering.

She's more to me than a mourn
in this fiber-built funeral shed

that holds these desolate faces who haven't
shown themselves in years.

They beg themselves to fool me of pity,
knowing when they leave, their lives, though
paused for this hour, will carry on.

As mine stays hugging this rose embroidered
casket,

*sweetly sealed with a daughter's sobs.*

*-creeping out of the woodwork*

*I wish your head hadn't been so loud*
*and the voices didn't break you.*

*I wish we could still drink red wine*
*and sing karaoke in the living room.*

*I wish you could stand in front of me*
*and see the warrior I have become.*

*I wish you could stand in front of me*
*and say,*

**"You did it all, and I couldn't be prouder."**

## The Rise of a Woman

A mother, a woman of mercy for the children she created inside of her. A woman who holds all the power of who her children grow into. A woman who knows nurture and instinct. To be held by a mother is to never feel unloved. The bond between mothers and children is one that can be impossible to break. But what if who had broken it was the one who held the power? The mother. The one that makes our heads feel better when they feel clogged with sickness. But what if the sickness is from the one who holds the nurture. The mother. The one who protects us from falling into danger. But what if the one who is dangerous is the one with instinct? The mother. How will I know who to run from when I am running towards the only one I am taught to run to. The mother. The one with all the power. The mother. The one who nurtures. The mother. The one with instinct.

I romanticize all the things that are bad for me because I was raised to believe I didn't deserve anything good.

The Rise of a Woman

A rage,
a whisper.
Regret,
remorse.
Freeze.
Move slower, move faster.
Soft spoken silence.
An itch that is burning,
creeping up my throat.
A realization
that here, now,
is an end.
A grievance,
a memory
of my mother is all that is left.

-*the quietest day*

Rhiannon Janae

My mother raised me
to fight all her inner battles.

The child I was,
put on all her armor,
weighing me down,
dragging on the floor.

My hands were too small
to carry her sword.

So, when she died,
I didn't blame myself
for fighting her battle.
I blamed myself
for not being able to win.

## The Rise of a Woman

My child tears looked so sparkly falling down my cheeks. If only my hands could have held something shiny inside of them, then maybe I wouldn't have become so unremarkably consumed with the darkness all around me. Maybe then, I would have been able to close my eyes and no longer be in fear.

*-when it started to become complex*

Rhiannon Janae

A sickness
breeds inside of me.

A hunger,
a madness
from hands that don't know how to love.

A haunting,
a hostage.
It's the only love I've known.

I want aching.
I need reckless.
I need a lover who's broken.

It's addicting.
It's consoling.
**It's all my parents ever taught.**

## The Rise of a Woman

*I pull roots from my mother out of my mouth.*

*Her cries that were silenced drool from my lips.*

*Her bruised hands that her father held too tightly*
*burn the palms of my own.*

*I am everything she couldn't become.*

*I am nothing she was.*

*I am a stem in her soil.*

*-and damnit I will grow*

The hunger inside of me is longing for a child. Not for me to bear, but for me to remember. The child was me. But now the child is lost, and I need to seek her to fill my insides with cleansing because I cannot sleep when she is missing. The bags under my eyes weigh heavy. Sometimes I can hear her weeping when the lights dim and the bugs swarm. Sometimes I can see her if I close my eyes and think of snow days in December, but I can't find a way to keep her. The hunger is becoming greater, the oceans under my eyes are flooding, and I do not want to starve this impending hunger anymore.

## The Rise of a Woman

I have lived my life in the shadow of my mother. Hiding myself from the sunshine so **they** can't see me. As much as I contort myself into the darkness, the light always creeps in. I am more than this. I am more than who **they** choose to see me as. I wasn't meant for their horror show. I was made for the *sunshine*.

*–the bloodline will drown me*

Rhiannon Janae

Restore me.
Release all the violence I'm covered in.

I always swore it was never "that" bad.
That all of us are born into misuse.

"I've seen others have it worse."

My father's new wife once told me after only
months of me having been paralyzed by seeing
my mother's death.

It wore me.
Part of me thinks it still does.
Under my skin,
beneath my bones.
My eyes still burn and cause me headaches.

But my father's wife was right all along.
"I've seen others have it worse."

Yes, I've seen it all.

*My mother dead before she ever chose to live.*

*I find comfort within chaos
because chaos is what I once
called home.*

Rhiannon Janae

I picture my mother young,
a child before the curse of adolescence or the
muffled dangers of the world broke her.

She once wore a smile so sincerely that it
brightened her own mother's day.
Basking in the sun,
becoming one with the earth.

*When did the day come when it all changed?*
*What hour did she turn on herself by drowning in*
*life's waves?*

I can see myself reaching out my hand for her
and becoming all she needs.

*But my arms aren't buoys,*
*and I am no savior.*

The sea, she and I are all one.
But if I stay, I am too scared of what the waves
might uncover. The tide is telling me to go, *or*
*we will both go under.*

# The Rise of a Woman

Guilt has been the effects of grief lodging inside of me, growing larger with taunts of how my hands could not do the one thing they were raised to do. Save.

*-I was raised to save*

Rhiannon Janae

My pulse strikes through me
like lightning before thunder.

There is a storm brewing inside of me
of memories I have buried deep below the
tragedy within me.

If I keep going on like this, I might go under
towards the darkness of my childhood.

Back into the arms of a mother who only knew
how to love the pieces of me that fit with hers.

I can feel the suppression, as the child within
me screams,

*"Stop trying to make yourself whole from the parts of
me you choose to take."*

But I withdrawal.
It's all just a memory.

## The Rise of a Woman

*She lives inside of me.*
*Grief is her name.*
*She wears me as hers,*
*embodied by all that she is.*
*I sink, I swim inside of her.*
*She holds rage, but cries oceans.*
*She might deny the most obvious of answers.*
*She clings against me like skin.*
*She is warmth and she is comfort.*
*She is all I have ever known.*
*She could be my mother because when I lost her, grief*
*became my home.*

*-my home, my comfort zone*

Rhiannon Janae

Childhood trauma tricks me.
Every time I feel I am healed,
I realize that I have fallen into
harmful, yet comforting arms.
Nestling into the common pain,
numbing my way into familiar patterns.

*-the chaos we come from*

## The Rise of a Woman

A picture to capture a moment when fear hadn't consumed her yet. Her smile was contagious before the world left her jaded. She was a woman with dreams who had her hands constantly reaching. She was a mother too soon she may have thought. A lover, a wife to someone who never caught her heart. A remembrance, a shelter for her memories to live inside of my head. She was a woman, a fighter, but the war came to an end.

-*surrender to the light*

My whole life I have been fighting against becoming like my mother. My biggest fear to date. I have gotten so lost in who I do not want to be, that I have since neglected who I am.

*That's where the real tragedy lies.*

# The Rise of a Woman

Am I just a mirror of my mother to them? The person I try so hard not to be like is the person they see me as. I am the child my mother bore in her stomach and gave life to. I am my father's child also, though I do not feel like it. I feel like a disease that spreads when I'm at the dinner table with his new family. I feel like years of regret as he sees my mother all over my face. I feel like I was created on false hopes of holding something together that was cracking all over the floor. All those sharp cuts appear on **my** skin. I am one to be able to see that we are all human, but where does the line get drawn? I am constantly being reprimanded for my mother's mistakes. I am constantly looked at as if she lives inside of me and is seeping out of my pores. The woman my father once loved or maybe even still does, though he harbors it in his bones, is the reason I am here on this earth. The troubles of life I was born into came from the love of my parents. Why must I feel guilty for simply existing? Sometimes we must grow out of the spaces we were born into, and the ones who put us there in the first place.

Rhiannon Janae

*They call me cold because*
*I have caged myself inside a wire fence.*
*But they do not acknowledge how many cuts have*
*bled to make it inside.*

## The Rise of a Woman

I am haunted by the loss of my mother, endlessly blaming myself for years that I should have done better, as if I could cure the sickness that entangled her.

As if I am the reason her father scorned his only child.

As if my hands were the only medicine to heal her.

All of this haunts me,

and I never get enough rest.

*-what keeps me up at night*

Rhiannon Janae

I have been punishing myself for simply
existing.

I have taunted myself, pulled myself under,
falling into arms of a lover too broken to fix.

But I kept picking up his pieces
as my own continued to break off.

I was created from brokenness
and that is all I have ever known.

I am a child of my parents' neglect.

I was created because they needed a reason to
forget their own demons, but instead, they just
grew them inside of me.

*-generational*

*My whole life I have been
searching for peace from
others' wars that they have
led me to.*

Rhiannon Janae

Grief wore me like a dress,
taking me out on the town
as it shifted me through rows of relatives who
turned their cheeks to my tears.
When I saw a glow in their eyes,
it allowed me to see how sinister their neglect
was.
I was grief's endless fashion.

*Grief wore me like a dress*
*still hanging up,*
*waiting to be returned.*

## The Rise of a Woman

I have bitten my tongue so hard throughout my whole life, that now it runs through others like a chainsaw.

*-massacre*

Rhiannon Janae

I cannot sleep without the television on.
The voices of familiarity.
The sound of my childhood echoing through,
the one my mother once lived inside of.
I can hear her laughing in the background of
the static.
The white noise embraces me like my mother
once had.
I keep the television on as I slowly drift
unconsciously.
The noise deceiving me into believing she is out
there laughing at the screen and over the static.

*-I cannot sleep without the television on*

## The Rise of a Woman

*It hangs inside of my stomach,*
*aching for a feeding*
*that will only last temporarily.*
*Starving for love*
*from the broken ones.*
*The words of the silent.*
*The touch of the barren.*
*When I don't feed it, my body starts to panic*
*and nausea creates a reality of abandonment.*
*A feeling that I try so hard to run from.*
*I look for it in the bodies*
*of those who also run from themselves.*
*A mutual ache*
*we both know well.*
*If I don't feed it*
*I will have to face it,*
*and if I face it,*
*I will have to feel it.*
*And I am hungry.*
*I am starving.*

*-codependency*

Rhiannon Janae

Sunbathed in the earth's memories,
tears dripping down my sun kissed cheeks.
The earth whispers stories through each sway
of the trees.

How many faces breezed upon this?

How many tears dripped in dismay?

Why do I feel so special, as if I'm the only one
appropriate for this task?

All the tears I've shed do not even compare to
what the earth has seen.

As Mother Nature holds me, I whimper,
longing for my own **mother's** nature.

*-the only mother I have now*

# The Rise of a Woman

My memories are almost like an old tape replaying in my head. The VHS kind that can pause, rewind, fast forward. But it's decades old and the film is too fuzzy to make out the picture. Just a movie I once watched inside my eyes, but it's too fuzzy to remember if it ever even happened at all.

## Rhiannon Janae

I hope when I see my mother on the other side, her arms are wide and inviting. I hope her eyes cry in victory of how proud her child has made her. I hope we find ourselves in a different kind of embrace that we never got to appreciate in our human form. I hope she tells me of all the rose gardens she has been hanging out in, and all the ways the universe changes its color. I hope she exuberates peace and has left her trauma buried in a grave far away. I imagine her showing me all her new ideas for all the books she will surely finish in her next life. I hope she understands now how beauty is so deep within us that no matter how our bodies grow or the way our face shapes, it will pour through us just by the way we love. I hope when I see my mother again, all I am reminded of is how much I have missed her, and how much more time we have together now.

## The Rise of a Woman

Fall heavy on us,
like the lies that swarm
through these tiny ears of ours.

Do you love us?

Can we know?

You put us here for your own entertainment,
but no one here is entertained.

*No one is just.*

All we do is bury our tiny heads in our tiny
hands, wondering where your love is.

Rhiannon Janae

Many years I have lost,
trying to hold others' wants and needs.
If only the child within me closed her eyes
to the danger lingering up ahead.

She was naïve but not dull.
Her mind was full of endless journeys to travel
and wishes that love would bloom inside of her.

But now she is me.
A mind full of endless disaster,
with writings of sempiternal nightmares
wilting in the death of love.

No, that child is no longer.
Only me who has aged.

*-three decades later*

## The Rise of a Woman

I cry for my mother to come back,
but she is happy there where she is,
inside of the universe.

So, the voice in my head tells me I am not
crying for her, *I am crying for me.*

Rhiannon Janae

Run deep.
Heavy on you like the steel
inside of your chest.

You remember who she was
but not who she is.
It's somewhere inside of your skull,
the memory of death.
She's the warden, the beast.
Falling apart limb by limb,
curse by curse inside of her skull.
She was your lover, your feast.
Heavy on you, now heavy on me.
A mother, a devil beautifully wrapped in her
father's mistakes.
She wore no evil but was destructive in a dress.
You don't speak of her
and she can't speak of you.
The petals inside of your fist,
the wilting of the family tree.

She was heavy on you
*and now heavy on me.*

*-the mother of your first three*

# The Rise of a Woman

I am trying to find the words to write, but lately I just find myself staring at a blank screen of whiteness. It reminds me of my mother and the day that I found her lying lifelessly in the bathtub. Her face white, like freshly fallen snow that has yet to be stepped in with the feet of screaming children. Or the paleness of a cloud that has not yet been threatened by the muddiness that the rain wants to paint the earth in. I can still see the face of myself, that twenty-two-year-old girl who never knew what horror was until she saw it fill the four walls of that bathroom. How her childhood home had now been replaced by a surreal living nightmare that had taken over her life. I was young and God was I innocent. But that day in August, I became someone I never knew could be inside of me. I became broken and newly built all at the same time. The walls started building higher and higher around me to guard against what other evil might come my way. I lost myself somewhere that day, and I have been trying for the past decade to find her again. Is she still inside those four walls of the bathroom, standing, shaking over the body of the woman that gave her life? Is she still crying out for her mother, begging for an answer she damn well knows she will never hear? Is she stuck in the abyss that I have left her in? Had I built these walls inside of me so fast, that I forgot to get her out? Or am I too scared of facing her? Am I running away from hearing her feelings pour out of her mouth? I have been running for a while now and I'm scared I have run so far that I can't get myself back. But she's in here, under all the wreckage I have left, inside the walls I have built. Isn't it time to set her free?

*-uncage her*

## The Rise of a Woman

*The salt, the skin.*

*I purify the damage within.*

*I swear this is healing,*

*when I become one with the sea*

*that floods inside of me.*

*I cry, I swear*

*for the child in me that had to bear*

*a burden of love*

*my parents never shared.*

*The salt on my skin*

*from all the tears I've shed*

*for all those who never cry for me.*

Rhiannon Janae

This sadness is my own doing.
I've been rotting away in deluded ideas,
in the hopes that I can find my mother's
redemption in others.
But I am only left more wounded.
A bird as prey.
*A child still left abandoned.*

*-the void left empty*

## The Rise of a Woman

Now all she is, is a memory, a still frame
of when I was young.

I keep her there, in a time
before all the hurt.
Before all the horror
of seeing the woman I once wanted to become
turn into the woman I pray I will never be.

*And we whimper still for her acceptance*

*-mother, may I?*

# The Rise of a Woman

Dissociation;

A feeling I have felt for years. My mind has become somewhat of a sin because I have not figured out a way to get out or a way to get in. I have become that child I left years ago in my family home. The girl with her mouth sewn shut as her mother spoke the words for her. The girl whose heart raced at the sound of her mother fighting with her father. The girl who thought her hands were meant for mending others, but just formed callouses on them instead. I see her, staring at me in the mirror as I drink what's left in this wine bottle, as I weep another night from not being able to save my mother.

*"No." she says,*

*"You could not save her but there's still time to save me."*

And in the end, she was just like me.

*My mother.*

**A woman.**
**A fighter.**

*A battle that had brewed inside of her.*

**And just because she had lost, that does not take away from how fucking hard she had fought.**

# The Rise of a Woman

I am finding myself a little unwell. My stomach
has been churning with thoughts of the past,
and what's even worse is that it gags at the
thought of the future. I am a home with no roof,
embedded in the soil with no shelter to protect.
I want to keep things out, but I always find
myself letting too much in. Why can't I learn
how to walk away from those who only make
me feel worse? The curse of my mother, maybe?
I always search for love in the ones whose
hearts are burnt. I always want shelter from
those who have no roof. When will I learn that
I will never fill my void with things that are
shallow? If I just swim deep, I will find comfort
in the depth. And if I just let them, the waves
can take me to the home that I have been trying
to call. If I just stop resisting the tides, they will
take me back to myself.

*So, I sail.*

Rhiannon Janae

The metal rusts around my neck.

*Break the chain, destroy the silence they keep.*

A lion hides within me with a silent roar that's
begging to be heard.

*Break the chain, destroy the silence they keep.*

For every child who was loved in denial.

*Break the chain, destroy the silence they keep.*

We are told to love those who made us,
even if they cause us pain, but the generational
silence is choking me.

So, I *break the chain*, unleash the lion,
and destroy the silence with my roar.

*-a lion's roar*

When I found her, my mother, the paleness of her face was calmed as if she had finally welcomed peace in and let it take her to a place of healing. Maybe it was in that moment my eyes had the chance to see her at her happiest, even if that moment became my darkest.

*Maybe in the end, death became her life.*

The Earth's Beauty,

The Earth's Disasters

## The Rise of Woman

You cannot mold me.
My body is not made of clay.
It is made of bones.
Your mold would break me.
And I am not meant to become pieces.

*-I am meant to be whole*

Rhiannon Janae

*They look at us (women)*
*as some kind of offering*
*for their bruised egos.*

*But my hands have already bled*
*from holding a man too high,*
*and my hands have already broken*
*from catching his fall.*

*I have become so unattainable*
*that I have trouble*
*keeping myself from running.*

# The Rise of Woman

Sing to me fallen lullabies
of yesterday's plundered dreams

that were stolen by enemies
wearing sinister grins
and checkered ties.

Watch me like a fallen star
whose burning footsteps
edge away at the passing
of heartache.

Paint me as a woman
who wears disaster on her back
as she trudges through endless forests
in hopes of discovering safety.

Speak of me as a whisper
so that the taste of evil silences my savor of
peace.

Sing for me for I cannot,
since I have been silenced
by those who wear the sinister smiles
and checkered ties.

*-a man's world*

Rhiannon Janae


Alas, your ship has sunken into the abyss of
oppressed forgiveness.
Your woman has been released back into her
real lover's arms.
You foolishly grinned at her as she begged for
her life at your feet.

The wind whispered defeat to the trees
as they forbid pity on you.

You played as the king with no crown,
threatening virgin heads to present you with
bows.
Now your throne has been ripped out from
under you
by a **warrior woman** and her karmic crown.

*-karma is a woman*

## The Rise of Woman

When they feel they are losing control, they feed with violence.

*-the ones with the power*

## Rhiannon Janae

It is cold in a world like this,
where men silence us
with hands full of power.

It is cold in a world like this,
where our skin is shamed
for simply breathing.

It is cold in a world like this,
where children are punished
for the adults mistakes.

*It is cold, this world.*

## The Rise of Woman

*Look at my palms.*
*They will not tell you how many years I have left.*
*They will tell you how many years I have lost.*

Rhiannon Janae

I stand tall, though insecure that my height is judged by those who want to defeat me. Their insecurities lash out on women who don't meet the standards of their delusions. My mouth is too loud to be considered submissive. I don't fit the part of a housewife. My hips are not meant to bear children because the only child I long for is the one I have lost inside of myself. I don't feel sexy. I just feel like me, and sometimes I don't even know what that means. And if I'm being honest, the only man I ever loved wounded me. But if I say that I have been jaded by a man I will then be judged and told that all men are not the same. So, I stand tall, more secure, turning off the sound of insecurity, tuning out the noise of those who will only criticize.

*-their critique is their own insecurity*

## The Rise of Woman

My heart,
she's an outlaw
to her own body.
She might kill me,
cutting through me like a machete.
She falls for ones that shatter her to pieces
as I am left to clean them up,
and I am no good at puzzles.
I cannot try to save them all,
and even if I do,
they will decide to crack her all over again.

*-my heart and her great fall*

## Rhiannon Janae

I am not "chosen".

I am not a woman with a mouth sewn shut.

My tongue is sharp,
knives as teeth,
clenched and bruising.

It is not for beauty, but for peace.

To beg to not be the drool dripping down their
mouths.

I have the body of a Goddess,
holding savior like organs inside.

My skin is my suit.
It is not to be borrowed
or tailored to fit.

*It is just the right armor
to fight this.*

## The Rise of Woman

What a cruel world,
a walking horror.
Fight to fight,
war on war.
Neighbors now become ones to fear.
Love has now become hollow under
discrimination.
Brutality equals power.
No solace,
no love.
Fight to fight,
war on war.

**What have we become?**

## Rhiannon Janae

We itch in the purgatory of life.
We come here with hopes of love
and become something we despise.

Could it be, we have all the lost the way?

Are we all fighting against what we should be
fighting for?

To be one with each other.

Instead, we fight with each other and then say
we are just another one scorned.

*-hell is on earth*

*The vanity in you eats away
at the humanity in me.*

## Rhiannon Janae

I bleed from those
who cut me.
Yet, here I am,
holding the knife
above my head.
Bleeding from the hands
my mother gave me,
passing it back
to brace for another wound.

## The Rise of Woman

It's in the earth's beauty
that we reminisce
about all the brilliant ones before us.
Honoring those
who were silenced before our cries,
who suffered before our rise.
The bodies of the holy.

It was in the bite of the apple
that we took back what is ours.

The crown of survival,
the earth's most beautiful.
*The women we rejoice.*

*If I am considered evil for whom I choose to love, then I think The Devil and I will get along just fine.*

*–love is love*

# The Rise of Woman

My man
hunted me for years,
harvesting my beating organ
to chew into,
to fill his hunger.
The void, never full.

My woman,
Goddess, she calls me,
warms me under blankets
when I get too cold.
Her love, overflowing.

Yet I'm still hunted
by men
who believe our love
is something vicious, evil.

We stand empty handed
with their daggers pointing at us.
We stand empty handed
as they call **us** inhumane.

*-the vicious, the vile*

*My*
*skeleton*
*is*
*not*
*yours*
*to*
*smolder*
*in your hands.*

*–unbreakable*

## The Rise of Woman

Today our rights were taken away by those
who don't even know we exist.

Those who don't know our struggles or how
our bodies function.

Those who deny care even if we breathe or if we
choke.

Those who are so hurt on the inside, they want
to demolish us.

Today we are no longer considered worthy
enough to have a choice about our future and
those who choose to help us will then live in
cages.

Today our independence as women was taken
away by those who don't even know our names.

*-Doomsday in June*

*A woman's body; a museum.*

*Do not touch.*

*It is art.*

*It is invitation only.*

*A woman's body; a temple.*

*Do not enter.*

*It is religion.*

*It is God.*

*It is only for believers.*

*A woman's body; an earth.*

*It is nature.*

*It is magic.*

*It is hers.*

# The Rise of Woman

This air was meant to be breathed in by all those who walk its planet. These roots were planted for the existence of all those who grow from it. Look at the way the moon cries now as it sees how hard our ancestors fought, only to regress hundreds of years later. Look how the sun gravels for the surrender of those to stop pointing their guns at its children. What have we done? How did we get here? How are we listening to men who hate that woman get to fight for their rights just to exist? How are we muddling through fallen bodies to justify our own riches? The soil we walk on has been embedded by footprints of resilient women who have fought for their voices and equality so their children could lay their heads on their beds in peace. The world has become masked with monsters who will eat away at others for the sake of their own hunger. But we are all worthy and we all come from the same soil. The universe bore us all into the same existence, yet there are those who take that away. It is a dog-eat-dog world, and so many innocent ones have now been born back into the sunset.

The comfort of a stranger, the quiet of the night. I long for a world where we catch the tears that fall from eyes that aren't our own. I cry for a world where we fight for each other and not against one another. I yearn for a world where the more we look at the sun, the richer we become. A world where the air we breathe is healing and not poisoned. A world where the words we speak come from our hearts and not the boiling of our blood. Where a stranger is a friend whom you haven't gotten to know yet. We have become maggots eating away at each other for the gain of our own famine. The beast within us gorges for more greed and becomes more evil inside. I long for a world where we fight for each other, not against one another.

*-if only*

## The Rise of Woman

*Sometimes I wish that I could treat others how they*
*treat me,*
*but this heart inside of me is too warm*
*and holds all this weight.*

*My empathy*
*will be the death of me.*

Rhiannon Janae

To judge someone who is broken is to deny
yourself of your own shattered pieces.

The Rise of Woman

I want to breathe
and feel the world
without the ache
it leaves on us,
or the hate
it spews out onto us.
If we could learn
to leave the earth be,
who could we become?
Who could we be,
*if we just let everyone else be?*

*-the human hate*

Rhiannon Janae

"Inhale."
they say,
as my whole chests lumps itself into torture.
I can feel my heart knocking at my chest,
begging me to release the secrets
I hide from myself
and from others.
I'm a disaster wrapped in counterfeit diamonds.
Pretty on the outside
but fake on the inside.
You can hold this bag to my mouth
and tell me to inhale.
But it's not the inhale that scares me,
it's the exhale.

-*what lies beneath*

*There's a sea of anger that*
*runs inside of me*
*and I am scared if I don't*
*tame its waves,*
*it will pull me under.*

Rhiannon Janae

Every morning

I wonder,

"Will today be life-changing, trauma run, slept
away, inspiring?"

I live in moments that haven't happened yet
instead of the moments that are happening.

Always looking too far ahead to things I cannot
see instead of the things right in front of my
eyes.

The eyes that have gone wandering.

*-wonder is for the worry*

## The Rise of Woman

What grows inside of me?
The anger that forms.

What grows inside of me?
The honey I bleed.

What grows inside of me?
The lover I grieve.

What grows inside of me?
The mother I seek.

What grows inside of me?
The many versions of me I will be.

Rhiannon Janae

I am calm in a storm, yet frantic in the silence. Surviving on the emotions I have felt as a child. Combative, always ready for war. So, please bring me the thunder, so I can feel this was all worth fighting for.

*-survival mode*

## The Rise of Woman

*In between hundreds of miles*
*inside my dreamlike state,*
*a scene these grey eyes*
*never thought they could gaze.*

*How romantic to wake*
*up to tides that*
*even the hummingbirds get*
*jealous of.*

*Highways that don't catch speed*
*and night skies*
*that dream in light.*

*Yeah, I think I like it here,*
*even if only to find it in my slumber.*

*Yeah,*
*I think I would love to become one with the Pacific.*

*-deep dreams, deep blue*

Rhiannon Janae

I have found myself graveling at sadness as it enters my body. I want to feel it all but also vacate it all. I am a tree, and my arms are branches that reach out and only come back with dirt and soil in their hands. How many times will I find myself digging the same old graves? I keep recovering the same bodies with the same stories. They fall into the dirt and soil, then leave their traces on my branches. It's the same motion day in and day out. How will my roots grow when I keep drowning them in my overdue heartache? The past keeps draping itself all around me and it's starting to block out the sun. I need to get out of myself to get back in. I need to let these burdens pass through me and drift down the stream of my river. It is no longer the past, so why do I feel like I must consume it? It haunts me like an old horror film, and I am the final girl. I find myself running around the same haunting thoughts that never quiet down. I have tried to squeeze these thoughts out of me, but my temples are just left bruised. How have I been captive to my own thoughts? "Let me out! Let me out!" I scream to myself, but my ears just spit my pleas back out at me, leaving me blushed. I find myself so unlovable sometimes and I fear my brain will never convince me otherwise. It locks me out and keeps the wheel away from me because I have steered it wrong so many times before. But I keep knocking, praying that at some point I can forgive myself. I keep knocking because I know how she is, she always gives more chances than deserved.

*-the final girl*

The struggle of not being able to let go of the ones I have lost is my tragedy. They beg for me to put them to rest, but I fear I am too selfish in my own grief to give them back to the earth.

## The Rise of Woman

I think I've been too silent. I have let my words become a part of my insides. Hiding, intertwining my grief behind the parts of me I hide from everyone. I think I've been too silent. I have let people take from me, filling themselves up as they leave me empty. I think I've been too silent. I have let my empathy drown me in others' grief, as my own grief is left unacknowledged. I think I've been too silent. I have let my power become attached to those who only want to take it. I think I've been too silent. I have let others determine who I should love and who I should become. I think it's time to let my absence speak much louder than my silence ever has.

*-watch me as I disappear*

Rhiannon Janae

*The moon and her power*
*will open the grief within us.*
*Evicting all that holds us back,*
*illustrating how we are meant to glow.*

## The Rise of Woman

There are pieces inside of me
that I've gathered along my ways.

Others' heartbreak that
I have let break my own.

Others' failures I have let
delay my own success.

Others' grief I have let
fill me up inside.

There are homes inside of
me that were never mine to house,
weighing me down
and pulling me under.

There are pieces of others
inside of me that I must release
in order to put my own back together.

-everyone I have ever loved still lives inside of me

I have fought so many
battles,
yet not all of them were
my wars.

## The Rise of Woman

It's been years, way over a decade since we found love in each other with our loud senses of humor. It was an instant bond, like we were destined to run around the city together and breathe in the relief of teenage freedom. It was perfect until it wasn't. I was crumbling inside of my mother's abuse. Day by day, year by year. I was becoming a version of myself that I had never met before. Fighting over boys, ruining our bodies for the sake of the mirror lying to us that it would make us beautiful. To this day, I keep trying to find you in others, but no other person has ever made me laugh the way you had. I wish I knew then what I know now. Then, maybe our friendship would still be growing, endlessly. I wish I knew how to love back then without seeing my mother's face on everyone else's body. Maybe one day, I will see you there, standing in front of me, with your smile scrunched to the left side of your face, and I can tell you I am sorry for not seeing your pain. I can tell you I'm sorry that it seemed so easy for me to walk away. But for now, I keep our memories closer than you'll ever know. And if this is all I'll ever get a chance to say, I want you to know how grateful I am to even have those memories.

*-the friendship that caused the most heartache*

Rhiannon Janae

Is it a curse to be strong?

My body feels heavy,
holding the weight of others.

The expectations are daunting.

I have walked miles in others' shoes
as my feet bleed.

Yet, still,
my feet keep moving.

*I know that somewhere deep inside of me is a thread holding onto all the ones I have said I let go of.*

Rhiannon Janae

The last of us.
The moon hung low
and devoured us in its arms.
When I look for you,
I let the stars point me there.
If I look close enough
I can see where the light held us.
It's your home now,
inside the moon's belly.
Make space for me.
When I'm done with the ground,
I'll return to the moon's belly
where it will once again light us.
I'll hang inside the moon's belly,
the home I return to when
I become too tired.
It will erase the mistakes that
kept my head hanging low
in this realm.
I'll return inside the moon's belly,
where I will finally feel full.

*-moon sweet moon*

## The Rise of Woman

I've been swimming in others' oceans
treading with them
as they weigh my body under waves.

I have held my breath so long
that I can almost forget the sound of my own
voice.

I am the captain of a boat that is always sinking
as the anchor wraps inside my hand.

If only I would just let go,
I could make it back to shore.

*-the anchor, the captain*

Rhiannon Janae

Why am I so upset with how everyone else treats me when I hate the way I treat myself? Am I the wolf in sheep's clothing? Am I the grenade that blows myself up? Are others learning how to treat me by the way I treat myself? Why the fuck do I keep getting treated as if I wasn't the one who took a chance on the ones that were broken? Broken people break things, and I am the pieces of that.

The Rise of Woman

I am a ship with no sail,
but I don't fear the waves
because I've been under the sea
my whole life.
Sinking and swimming
just to kiss the top.
And when I get there,
I will thank the sky for allowing
the air to open my lungs.
I will let my body gently move with the tide
as it gets closer to the shore.
It is not the shore that I fear.
What I fear is letting this anchor go that has
clung to my feet.
It holds a lifetime of pain and memories,
keeping me under the sea,
waiting for me to loosen it
and swim to shore.
One day, I swear,
when I get there
I will thank the sky for being patient
and the air for letting me cry.

## Rhiannon Janae

I would say that I am lonely, but the Moon and I stay up late together while others share deep hypnosis. She tells me about the many tears she has cleaned up from those who weep for her. She cries for God to answer those who plead for him when they look into her eyes. But he never answers, and those sorrowful heads become bitter under her light. She becomes lonely, blamed for battles she never could help fight. The Moon would say she is lonely, but she and I stay up late together, as I admire her abandoned light.

*-my sleepless nights under the moon*

# The Rise of Woman

*Close your eyes and tell me*
*I am much more beautiful*
*than what my skin has to offer.*

Unveil the mask that has sunken into my face as I disappear from the one who holds me. The mask that wears me out and comforts others. The smile they all see as a way of feeling better about themselves. This mouth that says words that fill others' egos. I want to rip this seal off my mouth and let the words ring through my ears as my last offering. I am done. I feel too big to fit in these tiny spaces. I feel too unheard to say any more words. What do you want from me, if you can't give anything back? What do I have that you need more of? I am made of the same insides of all, yet I keep feeling lighter and lighter as they take more from me. I have footprints along my ribcage and manipulation in my ears. Take this mask off my face, undo this ribbon that seals my lips. I am done. I am done. There is nothing left for you here.

## The Rise of Woman

My palm covers my mouth when I try to speak
of you.

The widow,
the warden,

the woman I've kept trapped inside.

The sickness,
the heartache,

the feelings I've let grow inside.

I am hiding behinds things I cannot face,
refusing to see you for who you were.

I am the widow,
the warden,
the sickness,
the heartache.

Holding onto what it could have been,
living in my own prison of what it was not.

Rhiannon Janae

When you see death,
it's hard to look at life without it.
I find myself often staring into the abyss of life,
clinging onto memories
with every inch of force from my fingertips.
Becoming so lost in the "what could have been"
that I find myself so still.
I wonder if I am here at all
or if there is part of me who has died
with them.
And that's what I have been grieving this whole
time,
*the lost parts of myself.*

The Rise of Woman

Throughout my life I've been fighting against myself, becoming my own enemy. I've intertwined myself with forces that I bend to break, to mold, to fit into me. I was taught that my needs were to be only meant for others. So, I break, mold, and fit them into me. I have loved so hard but have nothing to show for it. I am an endless tunnel trying to navigate out of this person they've created inside. How do I break free? How do I break free from the versions of myself others have created?

*-a version for all is a version for none*

Rhiannon Janae

My years have erased me. Somewhere inside this head of mine are memories that hide behind shadows and peek over darkness. Somewhere inside of me are cages of all the people I have ever loved that I can't find the courage to let go of. Somewhere inside of me are answers I am too afraid to hear for the sake of my inner child's denial. Somewhere inside of me lives someone who is gasping for air as I let the waves build higher. Somewhere inside of me is someone I am trying to dig out as I keep piling on more dirt. Somewhere inside of me lives all the things I have yet to uncover.

*-somewhere inside she lives*

## The Rise of Woman

I find comfort in the fact that the worst of my days are behind me, but why doesn't that stop me from fearing as I rear around the next corner?

*–post traumatic*

The sun reminds me that her light will always show up, regardless of how many days I choose not to see her.

# The Rise of Woman

A funeral
is a remembrance
of love that moves on.
Not faces that are unrecognizable,
blurring to memory.

Do not come for me
when I am gone
when you could not show up for me
while I was here.

Do not cry for me
when I become released
when you were vacant
while I was kept.

Do not love me because I am gone.

My goodbye is not your hello.

*-I am not a sympathy card*

## Rhiannon Janae

*When the sky cries on me*
*is when I feel most alive*
*because it reminds me*
*even the earth needs to let it out.*

## The Rise of Woman

It is in the ruins we are then reminded of the
strength we hold inside of our bones.

It is in our heartbreak that we feel how deeply
we have loved.

It is in the world's devastation that then we see,
finally, how beautiful life is.

*-bad gratitude*

I want to believe that all the pain we bear deep inside of us is just a child who needs to be told that they are enough. I want to believe that the bad in us is just a veil of insecurity that was given to us as children. The way we longed for our mothers to keep us warm, or how we looked to our fathers to show us how to love without expectation. I want to fill the child inside of me with words that she has been longing to hear to help her mind stop breaking at night. I want to take the rage of her and spread it out to make butterfly wings and let them fly into forgiveness. I want to believe that throughout all of our pain lies an ending that drifts the weight off our shoulders. I want the pain to fly with its wings as I become the love I was never shown.

*-to fly is to forgive*

# The Rise of Woman

I hope that with the time that passes I will see the world with compassion and not see the way we all roam around its beauty with such hate in our hearts. We all walk on soil that bleeds our ancestors as our ignorance fails to appreciate their growth. How cruelly the world must think of us, as we pollute it with smoke from engines to get us to and from our daily forms of hell. Oh, how I hope with more time that passes, the world accepts my awful doings of not showing enough thanks. I hope as more time passes, I can dig my heels into the dirt and learn from its beauty.

Rhiannon Janae

I have dug my feet in this soil and clawed my nails through the mud. The sweat. The blood. It pours down in the vanity the world projects. Keep me here, underwater, or plant my roots in the forest. The only beauty I seek now is the beauty of her, *Mother Nature.* A woman of mercy, battling the world of humans.

*-global harming*

## The Rise of Woman

I see her
after years without her.
She calls for me.

As I face her,
she reminds me of home,
the real place that I belong.

The home we forget about as we roam around
this disaster.

She sings,
and in her song
I remember all that I am
and all that I was.

Before I was the woman I've become.

She reminds me
that she is home.
She reminds me
she is the sun.

# The Rise

## The Rise of a Woman

*I will not become the one I am most afraid of.*
*I will become greater than that fear*
*and watch the scariest parts of myself*
*calm me back into existence.*

The one thing I beg myself every morning to conquer is my mind. The war that never quiets down. The waves that forever overflow. The fire that only spreads. *My mind.* It's a battle of love and hate. The self within. The grief we let build a wall within us, so incredibly sustainable that it seems almost impossible to climb. How can it be that we are both the hero and the villain within this flesh of ours? We must save ourselves from our own hands that hold us under. We must resist the urge to let ourselves be locked into this jail cell that we have created within. A prisoner of self. The worst kind to become. A crime with no trace and no justice to allow. How am I so afraid of becoming someone that is already living inside of me, breeding with every minute I give it thought. A monster that keeps me echoed inside of its walls. I must release myself from the resistance of my own thoughts. I must catch the fall of being pushed off the edge of my own tower. I want to embrace, abide and accept the mere being of who I am. So quiet down the voice inside, I am ready for war.

## The Rise of a Woman

A journey for oneself
can become a war within.

A battle we must fight to break bad habits
that were passed down to us from those who
never fought.

Consumption can overtake, threatening us to
become what we have been fighting against.

The anger that hungers us,
bubbling up to the surface to release our
demons.

One against one.

The war we fight
is the war to stay within ourselves.

To become the opposite of what we fear,
and not let fear become who we are.

It is not about what we have lost,
*but what we can still save.*

Rhiannon Janae

*At night when I can't sleep,*

*I imagine that I am a sunflower*

*trying to find the light to nourish my growth.*

## The Rise of a Woman

We must remind ourselves that the life we are living is magical. That it's turns and turbulences are pivots to put us back on track. It's okay to bleed and mourn all that we lose along the way, but we must keep on going. What's been lost will return. What once bled will now bloom. In the end we will be proud of the journey and the many miles we've traveled.

Rhiannon Janae

Strong, but senseless.
She was nothing short of desperate.
Gasping all over herself
for just a feeling,
just a moment,
just a breath
to claim herself back.

*-reclaim who lives inside*

Those who try to stunt your growth have already neglected their own garden.

Rhiannon Janae

I built my own tools
from the wreckage I was left in.
I produced my own water
to put out the flames that spread inside of me.
I ignited my own ability
to shed off the grief that has smothered what
has been left of me.

*-up in flames*

## The Rise of a Woman

I am in a constant battle of loving the woman I have become and hating who she used to be.

Rhiannon Janae

I am a woman with a violent mouth.
Sometimes my words cut through tongues
and burn like flames.
But I am also a woman of passion
and loyalty.
I will fight in your war
if you are loved by me
and I will slash your ego
if you do me wrong.
I am a woman of emotion
that echoes inside of me.
I hold journeys inside of my baggage.
I will love like no other
and I will keep you warm in my devotion.
I am a woman
who will see what you give back
after I've gifted you a part of my pieces.

# The Rise of a Woman

Sadness has become my strength. Reigning in over all the pieces of me I have lost along my way, sailing through my blood like flies to wine. I have become a thing some others may call heartbreaking. But that has become what binds my bones from cracking. The heartbreak inside of me has woken me up from what had been killing me slowly.

It wasn't love.

It was the lack of.

The shell had to be fixed

*and I held the hammer.*

Rhiannon Janae

*Am I just a reincarnated version of myself who is trying to fix the many versions that came before?*

## The Rise of a Woman

I must get off this rollercoaster I have buckled myself onto. Because after all these years, there is no one left on it but me. Yet, all I find myself doing is riding the same tracks, expecting myself to arrive somewhere else.

*-arriving at the same stop*

Rhiannon Janae

*I yearned for others to guide me as I ignored the map
that sat clenched in my own hands.*

## The Rise of a Woman

I am not out of tune; I just need to fix some organs I have let run me from the inside. I have been ignoring the gut in me that trembles when its triggered and tries its best to speak over the voices in my head that tell it to shut up. See, I know where I got lost along the way, but it was never about the end, it was always about the journey. I have been walking on top of eggshells as they crack and slice my feet. But the sores tell a story. I slept in a bed with an enemy and kept listening for honest words, knowing they would all be fiction. See, I don't need to be fixed, I just need to deny my empathy from pulling me towards those who want to wreck my self-worth. No, see, I am not broken, I am just chipped. I am learning how to sew myself up from the inside out. I am not damaged goods; I am an open cut that has never bled out and keeps fighting to heal. I will always be a work in progress because I will never give up on myself. I will always want to be better than the woman I was before her. I will always want to become kinder than the woman I was before her. I am not out of tune; I just need to fix some organs inside of me.

*-fix-er-up-her*

Rhiannon Janae

*The person I keep looking for is the same person I keep running away from.*

*-myself*

## The Rise of a Woman

I have held grief on my back
for decades.
Shushing it back into the darkness
until the day I was ready to face it.
It flourished under the moonlight
I hid in
and the hole inside of me
grew larger.
I became someone who I grew to hate.
I could hear the woman I hid inside of me
whisper when it was quiet.
I didn't listen,
but she waited.
Then the day came
when I shut the echoes off
and that's when she told me,

*"You will never feel redemption until you stop
blaming me for what others have chosen to do."*

You deserve a love who does not keep you in a constant state of survival mode.

# The Rise of a Woman

Maybe life gives us pain because it wants us to find peace overwhelming. Maybe it throws us in the riptide, so we learn to love the lightness of the waves. The calm comes after the chaos. The sun comes after the storm. So that now, as all the hurt has quieted down, we can enjoy the sound of silence.

Rhiannon Janae

I no longer want to shrink myself to fit in your
tiny spaces, but to stand tall is to no longer
bend my back for the ones I love most.

## The Rise of a Woman

The knot
deep inside of my stomach
fills with words
I will never get to say
to people I'll never get to see,
here at least.

So, I write and write
until it all makes sense,
that these words were never meant for them.

They were meant for a woman
who's been asleep,
who needs to wake.

So, I write and I write
so the knots can unravel
and the pain can settle.

Then she will see
these words are meant for *her*.

I will no longer feed my
soul to those who only
want to feed themselves.

*-I'm full*

## The Rise of a Woman

Remember me,
I say to myself,
as the younger me
becomes swallowed
by the warrior I have become.

Remember me,
I say to myself,
*for a seed cannot bloom*
*without its soil.*

*-woman in transit*

Rhiannon Janae

Please let me exist through all of my failures,
because without them, I would never have
appreciated the warmth of my success.

## The Rise of a Woman

*I have experienced so many wars inside of myself.*
Though I am bruised, I am resilient.
Though I am scarred, I am clean.
There is a machine inside of me that picks me
up and keeps me going.
There is a machine inside of me.
**I am built to last.**

*-woman tough*

Rhiannon Janae

*It's strange to see what happens when you start to love yourself.*

*You start to smile at the things that once had you in tears.*

*I will no longer extend these arms of mine to those who don't know how to reach back.*

I show growth when I let go of things that no longer suit me.

## The Rise of a Woman

I know her.
I can recognize her smile.
It reminds me of days under the sun
immersed in knee-deep waters.
Cleansed, clean,
untouched by pain
because it was too unknown.
Naïve, sarcastic,
telling jokes so they would heal wounds.
I know her.
She reminds me of birth and innocence
that I never meant to give up.
I know her.
I know,
her.

*-she is me*

Rhiannon Janae

I will no longer live **my** life fighting for **others**
when the **others** live their lives fighting **me**.

*-one way street*

## The Rise of a Woman

Healing is a journey that takes time and courage. Breaking down while healing does not show weakness, but strength in the fact that we have finally dove deep enough into the waters we were once only treading in.

When things don't work out, we tend to panic and look toward others to fix us instead of healing ourselves. If we continue to look toward others to fix us, then we will continue to feel broken. You are the only one that holds the tools to fix what's inside.

## The Rise of a Woman

*I think I am starting to like the way I fit into my
bones.*

True beauty is shown in the fact that you have continued choosing yourself repeatedly, regardless of the hurt caused by the ones who have decided not to choose you at all.

## The Rise of a Woman

I will not let myself go under the waters that others have flooded inside of me. The weight of their burdens that I have carried with me for years only slow my footsteps. I am consuming myself with mistakes that I have never made or grief that I've never felt. Why must my hands catch others' tears as my own fall onto my lap? Why must my shoulders hold the weight of others when my head falls into my own hands? I am the woman they call when they need comfort, but I shiver at night. I am the woman they can count on as I stare in the corner and bite my nails as I wait for the pain to pass. I am the woman that never lets anyone down as I sit alone, sinking further and further into my mattress. They say you get what you give, but all I do is give everything and become empty handed. So, I'll shut my mouth and still my head, and ask myself to give to me what I give to others.

Rhiannon Janae

*To be brave is to continue fighting*
*through the things that are trying to*
*destroy you.*

## The Rise of a Woman

I imagine that sometimes in life when we feel lost, we are trying to find the parts of us that we have lost along the way. Maybe when we feel a sense of loss, it's because slowly, life chips away at the parts of us that we no longer need. The parts that we have outgrown. Maybe, what we tend to grieve are the parts of us that we have lost through the battles of aging. It's funny how I've become so fixated on the etching pain of the grief I have for the loss of others but forget about the grief of all the many versions of myself I have lost. The child I once was that I have let escape from my memory. The late teenager I had sacrificed for the sake of my mother's happiness. The young woman I have let crack in the hands of a man who didn't appreciate the glass she was made of. I have become so consumed with wanting someone else to make me feel whole that I have let myself fall through my own hands. It is why the grief inside of me won't dissipate. I keep looking for something that isn't meant for me. I keep running around in circles, chasing myself until I can't catch my breath any longer. It is me that I need to mourn. It is me that I need to grieve. It is me that I need to let go of; the parts of myself that no longer suit me. It is only then that I will truly feel whole.

*Fix your broken pieces and see how much better you work.*

## The Rise of a Woman

*It is in this body of mine*

I have felt a shatter, a shine.

The calm, the chaos.

A love, a hate.

*It is in this body of mine*

I have felt at home and alone.

The shell I hide inside of

mockingly, ungrateful.

What a fool

I have been

to not love

*my asylum, my skin.*

Rhiannon Janae

"What would you do if you could go back?" she
asks.

*"I would have held on tighter and loved a bit less."*

## The Rise of a Woman

Today I shut the world out
because I needed rest
to become one with the woman inside of me.
To listen to her cries
and mend her grief.
The woman who has gotten me this far
in a life full of battles.
Today I shut the world out
to catch a breath
for the woman who has held me
inside of this body I have wrecked and abused
for the sake of control.
Today I shut the world out
because the woman inside of me
needs to rest.

*Ask her, the woman inside, why all the strength she has gained becomes forgotten when the pain seeps in.*

## The Rise of a Woman

Sometimes I get lost as I look out my window, wondering if there are bits and pieces of my old self floating around. I wonder if the old sadness I once drowned in is now a buried seed waiting for spring to come for it to be reborn into beauty. I wonder if the grief I used to let run me is now out among the clouds that hover over my tiny apartment, hiding the sun from blinding my eyes as I leave. I wonder how many old painful pieces of me have now become the things I find the most beauty in.

-*the beauty found in the pain*

Rhiannon Janae

The beauty you hold within yourself is the
magic that will change the path you are on.

## The Rise of a Woman

*I may never be healed,*
*but I will always continue healing.*

*I may never be perfect,*
*but I will always continue evolving.*

*I may never be liked,*
*but I will always continue loving.*

*I shall never be destroyed.*
*I will always continue existing.*

## Rhiannon Janae

I have found myself in love with another.
Her pieces shatter but cling tightly to her skin.

Could this be another tragedy?
Is our love meant only to destroy?

She calms me, but I've been here before.

Her hands are softer and tightly woven around
mine.

She doesn't let them fall.

Why be ashamed to love someone who is
broken when that's all I have ever been?

So, I watch her as her stem finds roots inside of
my words.

I tell her,

*"Listen to the sun and grow until you reach her."*

*Believe in yourself just as much as you fought to believe in all the wrong ones that weren't you.*

Rhiannon Janae

Let me shed my skin as many times as need be. Let me change my mind with the direction the wind blows. Let me find forgiveness for myself over and over as long as need be. Let me learn to love the parts of myself that I once hated. Let me be, let me be whatever it is I need to be.

## The Rise of a Woman

"When I grow up."
But it never comes
because my soul keeps on growing.
And when it stops,
it is not here that I will be.
It is in an infinite world with unlimited space
and I can assure you that even there,
*I'll choose to keep growing.*

Rhiannon Janae

Be still, the trauma inside.

I have lit a flame that will destroy all
those who hurt me that still live
within.

*-let it go up in flames*

## The Rise of a Woman

*The light inside of me has dimmed.*
*It waits for me to reach in and pull it through.*

*It's not the first time I have let myself become lost.*

*But I always return.*

*Sometimes I must walk away from myself*
*to appreciate all that I am.*

Rhiannon Janae

The sky got brighter the day I chose to open myself up and watch the past go. Something about healing makes the sun sing and the moon dance. Something about healing makes me want to dig my feet inside the earth's soil and grow as high as the trees. Something about healing makes me grateful that Mother Nature has gifted me the chance to become the one I was put here to be.

*-healing makes me dance*

The Rise of a Woman

*How could I have ever hated who I've been*
*when she is the very reason I am whole now?*

Rhiannon Janae

Now I no longer fear when a storm starts
brewing inside of me,
because it takes out all the unkept pain.

So, when it clears
I am left
cleaner,
lighter,
a better me.

No, you cannot tame me.

I am magic.

I am soil.

I am seeds.

I am growth.

There is no room for me hidden inside of your palms.

*I belong to the sun.*

Rhiannon Janae

I took all the broken pieces of myself and built a woman out of them. So now, when a battle calls, she will fight because she has already risen from all that was broken.

*-she comes back stronger*

## The Rise of a Woman

Here I am, digging my own grave, crying rivers and drowning my own bones. I harm myself every time I let thoughts of terror creep inside of my head and take over my entire body. I harm myself when I let people keep taking parts of me that I know they will never give back. I harm myself when I root my love into people that have hearts made of stone. I harm myself when I shame the way my skin folds on my body as I stand in front of the mirror. I harm myself when I let my lips seal and let others force opinions into them. I harm myself when I refuse to nurture my body or thank the spirit inside of me who fights every day to stay afloat. I want to come clean. I want to be acquitted of the sins I've committed against myself. So, I dig the shovel in the ground and throw seeds into the grave. I use the river of my tears to water the soil and wait for the bloom.

*-I am becoming my own hero*

*I evolve,*
*and I will love the parts of*
*myself I become*
*as much as the parts of*
*myself I have shed.*

## The Rise of a Woman

*I will tell you what I have learned the most throughout this journey:*

Searching for someone to fix your insides will only lead to more brokenness. That twenty-two-year-old girl who needed to hear those words lives deep down inside of me, somewhere, slumbering till she feels rested. She has fought battles that I can't even stand to think about. Her tears have washed over oceans and swept under waves. I am stunned she has made it back inside of me. So, when all this is said and done, what I really need to do is shut my mouth. Because this woman who I am now, lives in bliss thanks to her. So, I'll let her sleep so she can rise back. But for now, I will hold the sword she has left me, and make sure it is polished for her glorious return.

*But for now, I will just let her sleep.*

*-sleeping beauty*

## Rhiannon Janae

I have given my body to hands that couldn't mend it.

Hands that tore it down and used it.

I have given my heart to a heart that couldn't love it.

A heart that had many others inside of it.

I have given my twenties to someone who didn't deserve it.

*I have given, I have fallen, and I have risen.*

## The Rise of a Woman

Sometimes, what I see in the mirror staring back at me is a war of a woman who has gone mad. Sometimes I see a warrior carrying bodies on her back trying to get them to the finish line. Other times, I see a lion about to roar over those who resemble the pain of her past. But mostly, what I see in the mirror is a woman of survival and all the things she's conquered.

*-I will love the woman I am*

Listen to the woman inside of you, for she has fought all those inner wars for your survival.

## The Rise of a Woman

A smell.
A feeling
of nostalgia
of a life you once lived,
inside of a person you once were.
The bad was heavy
but the good was sweet.
I cry for her,
the child in me.
I want to connect
but it's all so *grey*.
An image of someone
who once breathed in and out,
just like I am today.
I cry for her,
but I know she's okay
because her roots have grown
and the heaviness has now decayed.

*-she is safe now*

## Rhiannon Janae

Who will you uncover when you stop being the
person they all want you to be?

Who will surface once the wounds heal and
their blades no longer cut?

Who will she be when you let her rise?

*Nurture the one who lives inside of you.*

Rhiannon Janae

I never believed I could heal. I started to believe I was just meant to hibernate under the rock I had created above myself. The darkness I had believed was my protection was only just a wound that was kept unclean. Love is cruel but it is also an awakening. If I had never loved him, then how would I have known I didn't love myself? If I had never lost him, then how would I have known that what I needed most was to find myself? I was a bird in a cage left unfed. A woman with a silent tongue, itching to scream loud enough for help. I can hear the voice in my head speak as I, for the first time, decide to listen. I don't want to be a stranger to myself. I don't want to keep dimming the light inside of me. I release myself from my own torture. I am not a burden or an outlaw. I am a woman who knows pain and strength. I am a woman who can see her own footsteps as a part of a journey she needed to walk through. I am endlessly growing and forever learning. I am not to be compared to another. I am a strange, yet unique kind of gem who allows other strengths and weaknesses to cling on as a remembrance. I now see that life sometimes gives you things you do not understand at first but will find gratitude in later. I have kept my head between my legs, hanging low in the comfort of depression. Why? Maybe because it's all I've ever known. Before I knew what depression was, I could feel it ooze off my mother's embrace. I could recognize it in my father's unreciprocated love for my mother. I could see it on my sister's cut up wrists. I could taste it in the food I stuffed inside my fragile body. I cannot leave this world with my soul wanting more. I want to leave this world with the feeling that I have done all that I've wanted. I want to see all that my eyes were meant to lay upon. I want to breathe air that I have never let my lungs inhale. I am somewhat of a storybook. I hold chapters of the years that have passed. But my book isn't done, and these pages must turn. The color is getting brighter, and the rain doesn't pain me anymore. I am grateful for the sun and for when she decides to rest. I have run marathons that I've never stepped foot inside. I am taking off the burdens that I have carried on my back for years and I am putting them to rest. The only weight I need to carry is my own. I celebrate the woman I am becoming because she is worth talking about.

*Though I have lost many lives in this life,*

*I will have many greeters in the next.*

## The Rise of a Woman

I am a warrior,
a weaver
of memories.

I am a child
trapped inside of a woman,
crying, screaming
for the home she has lost.

I am a monster,
a martyr
with anger that has grown
and swelled itself inside of me.

I am a spider
tangled in webs
of a lost lover and a lost mother.

I am a friend
and a lover,
balancing on the edge of solitary.

I am a warrior,
a woman
fighting until the end.

Regret is something I will no longer feel, for every step I've chosen has led me to something I've grown from.

## The Rise of a Woman

I felt a change, a release
as I let the anger filter out of me.

I felt waves
flooding out through my skin and eyelids.

I took a breath
and felt the grief exhale.

It stung a bit,
to accept that all of what I once wanted was
now over.

But a new beginning was overflowing the air
around me.

In that moment I felt alive,
breaking out of my old shell.

It was unknown, but all I ever needed to know.

It was a lifetime it felt since I allowed
myself to give in and let go.

And ever since, I have never looked back.

*-the day I chose to be happy*

Rhiannon Janae

Three decades and what have I gained?

The comfort of knowing that the woman I am
can ascend and rise, despite all the loss that
came her way.

## The Rise of a Woman

I wish I could see all the versions of myself that I once was, lined up against the wall. I would walk over to every single one of them and thank them for not giving up when I knew they wanted to.

-*your weakness is your strength*

I fear that abandonment will come back to get me. That it lingers in the dark corners of my room when I am sleeping, waiting to bring me back to it. A friend that I have known since I was young, who always wrapped me tightly in its arms. I have felt it creeping around me since, waiting to take someone else away from me, so I can fall back in its grip. Leave me be, I tell it. I have grown older, and I no longer need the cold embrace it gives me. It doesn't listen. It begs for my return as it watches me in my happiest moments. Dying to steal the joy I have worked immensely to feel. I see you, abandonment, at every corner, looming around, waiting for me to give you back my hand. But I have no vacant room inside anymore for you, abandonment. Because wherever I go, and whoever leaves, I will always have someone with me, and she is a hell of a woman.

*I hope when you leave this world, the proudest person is the one who is living within you.*

# Rhiannon Janae

If I could go back, I would tell my child self to hold onto the moments that don't hurt and to speak about the ones that do. I would thank my mother for trying her best even when she was at her worst. I would capture the clouds in the blue sky and apologize for the pollution they face. I would sit outside all day and appreciate the fact that we only rely on the beauty Mother Nature gifts us for our entertainment. I would ask the butterflies I caught in my hand, "Who's loved one are you looking to comfort today?" I would tell my sister she doesn't have to grow up so fast and that I need her more than she knows. I would watch my father more closely and observe all his pain so I could understand the man he grew into. I would encourage him not to ignore all the forks in the road, but to learn how to work through them. I would sing along with my little brother instead of snapping my tongue at him. I would beg my family to tell each other how much we love one another more often. I would float in water and appreciate how it doesn't trigger me yet. I would remind myself that my true beauty is in my fingertips and who I've always been is found in my words.

## The Rise of a Woman

"It is time." she says.

So, I take my sword
with others' battle wounds still dripping from it
and cut through the wars inside,
as I watch them bleed from me.

Finally,
I am reborn.

Rhiannon Janae

Fill me up
to the brim.
I'll overflow
to let you in.
Poison loves me,
it calms my grief
until I cry
myself to sleep.
Just like my mother said,
"This is as good as it gets."
Even though all I've ever known
has died and left.
Except the seed inside of me
that begs and pleads
for me to feed.
The time is now,
I've come this far.
So, I armor up
and grab my sword.
The war is within,
this I now see.
Fighting against
all the versions of me.
I will not kill
the ones I think I don't need.
Because this war is about
learning to be the woman I was meant to be.

*-a war inside of a woman*

*And in the end,*
*the story never tells of only*
***what** you have lost,*
*but all that you became*
***despite** all that you have*
*lost.*

Rhiannon Janae

She's in there.

Under the aching,
beneath the bruising,
embedded in the bones that hold you.

She's in there.

The one that knows all of this is worth it.

The fighter,
the empress.
The one who got you this far.

She's in there.

Under all the pieces others have broken.

Let her rise.
Let her surface.

The fighter,
the lover.

The one who you've been this whole time.

Let her in.
**Let her rise.**

-*the rise of a woman*

*And maybe it was the battles she overcame that made her so beautiful.*

## About the Author

Rhiannon Janae is a queer author residing with her girlfriend in New Jersey. She has two other self-published poetry series; *Words You Never Thought You'd Hear* and *Let Me F\*cking Cry*. She advocates for those who struggle with grief, like herself. Her work is vulnerable and raw. Her words dive into the depths of loss. She hopes those who struggle can find some sense of comfort through her writings.

Made in United States
Orlando, FL
04 September 2024

51152915R00171